Cobra.

Scott 1781 7

Gruce 1 617 968 0322
Qd - 510 -350 - 0716

Keri Apr Sgl

***

Luckland

Cover art by Jeff Weispfenning.

Back cover photo of the author by Edgar Sierra.

Some of the poems in this collection have appeared in other publications. Grateful acknowledgments go to: "A River That No One Mentions," Rising Waters; "To Rimbaud," Confrontation; "The Mystery of Pigeons Feeding In December," Cimarron Review; "Red Like The Wind," Snow Monkey; "Crows At Dusk In the Park," Puerto Del Sol; "The Weak Man," Poet Lore; "50 White Envelopes," Naked Knuckle; "Element of Shame," Controlled Burn; "Bigfoot, My Love," Powhatan Review; "The Old Man's Coat," Blue Unicorn; "Attempted Suicide, Sedalia, Missouri," Tar Wolf Review; "October Poem," Quercus Review; "Theory & Oblivion In The Writing Of Contemporary Poetry," The Mid-America Poetry Review; "From The Dead-End Tavern," Powhatan Review; "To Take It There" and "The Day I Killed Bigfoot," Out Of Our; "The Ice Cream Man Is Burning," "On The East Bank Of The Mississippi River, New Orleans," and "The Magical," Ijagun Review; "Because It Never Ends," The Bicycle Review; "The Dog In The Boat," The Maple Leaf Rag; "On Being Asked Again For Something By Someone I Didn't Know," The Cape Rock.

Published by Portals Press
New Orleans, LA
www.portalspress.com

Luckland **by Paul Benton**
ISBN 978-0-9970666-3-0

Table of Contents

The Dog in the Boat   11
A River That No One Mentions   13
To Rimbaud   14
The Mystery of Pigeons Feeding In December   15
Red Like The Wind   16
Crows At Dusk In The Park   18
The Weak Man   19
Fifty White Envelopes   21
Element Of Shame   22
Bigfoot, My Love   23
Another Recipe   24
This Transitional Life   25
The Old Man's Coat   26
The End Of The Day   27
There Are Dreams   28
The Haunted House   29
For Lennon   31
Attempted Suicide   32
The Fireplace   34
Rimbaud's Mother   35
October Poem   36
Theory & Oblivion In The Writing   37
There Is A Question   38
From The Dead-End Tavern   39
Lullaby   40-50

Other Dimensional Beings   53
On Being Asked Again For Something   54
Disturbing Messages   55
Heavenly Hill   56
Dear Mr. Benton   57
The Bitter Man   58
Sonnet (Bicycling Home After Work)   59
Popcorn   60
The Nail   61
To Take It There   62
Electronic Telepathy   63
Drinks Are Free   64
Hello, There Is No Hope   65

Found Poem   66
Bigfoot In The Mojave   67
Yesterday The Fortune Teller Was Crying   68
XXX   69
Lost (Decatur Street)   70
That Wide, Open Feeling   71
Bourbon Street, After Work   72
The Lazy Man   73
The Ice Cream Man Is On Fire   75
The Magical   77
You Have Won   78
Shoes   79
The Bee   81
Valentino   82
The Death Of Numbers   83
Orson Welles In "Touch of Evil"   84
On The East Bank Of The Mississippi River   86
Epitaph   87
The Day I Killed Bigfoot   88
The Lost Man   89
87 Questions   90
Charles Baudelaire   91
Hart Crane   92
John Berryman   93
Paul Celan   94
The Drunk Man   95
We Celebrate   96
Sit   97
Because It Never Ends   98
Drift   99

No Crime Was Committed   103
The Map Is Uncertain   106
The Drunk And His Three-Legged Dog   108
The Ugly Man   110
Little Yellow Flowers   111
Teen Age   112
My Grandfather's Accident   113
Together   114
October   115
The Window Washer   116

Kung Fu From Beyond The Grave   117
The Trees Fight The Sky   118
Lyric   119
The Guilty   120
2 November 2015   121
Lament   122
Doomsday Clock Now Three Minutes To Midnight   123
Live To Forget   125
Castle Of Monsters   126
Tomorrow Shoes 127
Vision   129
For Dave   130
French Quarter Sketch   131
The Fishing Pole 132
Bigfoot At 55   132
The Trick   133
Neighbors   134
What Do You Want   136
Godzilla Is Dead   137
The Sun-Light In Her Hair, His Tattooed Arms   138
Letter My Mother Kept   143
The Monkees   144
300 Years   145

Foreword

Paul Benton has actively honed his craft as a poet for over forty years. I've known him for all of that time. We share the same origin story of growing up in a small city in Missouri, defined by a handful of restaurants, a drive-in theater, and a single public high school where we became friends in a long ago creative writing class. Ever since then we've shared writing and life experiences, performed on stage together, and even shared a mobile home on the outskirts of a college town where we pursued our respective degrees.

Paul has gone on to publish his insights in dozens of respected journals and poetry periodicals. He has a natural knack of transforming the ordinary into the extraordinary, and I'll venture that you'll be moved to feel, to laugh, to think and maybe to cry when you read his poems.

I'm not a scholar of poetry, but I love how poetry can shape our emotions and mind's eye to feel and think about the world we share. That experience of emotion and vision may unite us in common understanding or shared memory, dark or bright, or it may introduce new experiences, new people and places you might not otherwise encounter. So, if you like poetry or books with remarkable imagery, dark realities, humor, and truths that will remind you of your own humanity and that of others, read on.

Ted Tennison
Tucson, Arizona

Luckland

Dedication

To Rodney Tullis
(1960-1993)
Friend and Poet

***

The Dog in the Boat

It was true, even if truth wasn't
the most important element,
true that there was a dog in a boat
rendered by someone's hand,
arranged and placed onto paper,
confined there and surrounded
by a simple black plastic frame —
a dog stands, forward-looking,
as it travels down a stream —
a multi-colored paisley body
of swirling water, pure
green trees and vegetation
line the banks. The dog's gaze
is set, eyes on fire with a distant sunrise,
sundown. What is the river's name?
The dog could not read those signs,
but each wave that kicked into
the side of the boat surely added
meaning and definition to the scene.

We would look at this picture
of the dog in the boat
and discuss the unknown future
as our sun rose and set
framed in that small room's
kitchen window, Vietnamese
voices spilling in from down the hall —
children playing games —
our words, our voices (sober or drunk)
navigated this limited space
day after day, and the dog in the boat

behind us, beyond us,
illuminated by what was approaching.

Some days we would place the dog
in the boat away, there in the closet
as if testing our own philosophy,
but nothing really changed.
We carried on our conversations
in the quiet world, points being made,
then other ideas raised.
No, nothing was ever solved:
then we'd decide it was time
to bring back out the dog in the boat,
it was time we'd both agree.

What kind of dog was it?
It seemed to be all dogs,
the common dog with its
classic stance in the middle
of shifting terrain, fortified
by its dogness. We'd stand there
and drink the image in,
refreshed — this one canine,
eyes unblinking as it straddled
the rocking vessel, going somewhere.

A River That No One Mentions

We barely sleep at all, but when we do
the dreams that come are trees
dividing thick darkness. Plain laughter

awakens us and we grab our guns,
holding them close like lovers that might,
if hugged too tightly, betray that love.

Each morning we yawn and walk to a window,
expecting the worst.

There isn't much left here, wherever this is.
No way to stop this thing that isn't quite war.

Scavenger birds pick flowers placed over our dead
and fly them away to who-knows-where.
This is our home and we laugh.

What has been left us
washes up daily against the banks
of a river that no one mentions by name.

To Rimbaud

My feet, look: they are cold in this cold room
where clocks won't tick and dogs kick at fleas,
raising gray dust toward heaven. I've come
to this tiny spot where sunlight is sliced
by these venetian blinds -- bars of gold shivering
through our wasted air, a movie I could
have watched before, late at night, in a dream,
the whole world black, white and almost solid.
And as these demons, these fairies, cavort down
musty hallways, books keep our secrets true.

My hands, look, they hold a wilted flower bathed
in light, a thing still white, but now this room is
awfully cold -- and I've seen God, and God
is growing old.

The Mystery Of Pigeons Feeding In December

You know it is the cold black earth, the sparse
grass beneath naked trees since late October,
the north wind attacking storm windows,
creation of a bitter language, cold syllables --
from a tongue of warning, many warnings,
all stress and churn, and this face in the window
framed in condensation, the face, male or
female, peering out through frozen glass --
rhythm of breath animates, obfuscates
the smeared and runny eyes that watch pigeons
peck at cold gravel. It is early morning,
cloudy; the weatherman calls for snow but
dusk will soon arrive with no snow in sight.
Downtown will be covered in a milky fog,
these pigeons elsewhere, cooing
beneath anonymous eves, dreaming of wasps,
spider webs.   You know it is impossible,
but it is, anyway, here: this mystery of pigeons
feeding in December, not a song, but song-like,
a brittle observation that hangs, a knife
of ice from the branch of a tree. You walk
by and see these pigeons, the face behind
glass; you begin counting the steps you take,
you are walking faster, you hold
your breath -- almost wanting to look back --
but no, you think, that would not be a good idea at all.

Red Like The Wind

for JW

Passed the Van Gogh, the Monet, the Magritte,
and passed the Picasso and the Kirchner,
passed them all, she comes here, again
and again, to this museum where I work,
every day near closing and begins
to circle a gallery, always dressed in the same
red pants, you can see her coming two blocks away.

What kind of animal march is this? Raw
and shuffling, flames no one can see must
burn beneath her feet, past Van Gogh's
amputated lobe, all this color squirming
around her as she lifts each foot, as each

foot falls, her mouth a white hot monologue of
monosyllables, a rhythmic stream,
the foundation upon which she propels
herself, and these sounds announce her
entrance, her exit, and her existence

"van gog, van gog, van gog," she says,
or something like that, and on and on,
her chant rolls out, and an old lady
in a yellow hat looks up in disapproval,
and a college girl laughs into her hands,

and the sound becomes a wave
that carries itself outward,
slapping up against those ruined
beaches where sunbathing
is no longer allowed,

16

and the last gull's cry
was heard somewhere above
in that lost blue
an awfully long time ago.

Crows At Dusk In The Park

after Georg Trakl

Gathering on the ground to feed,
from a distance they are black dots
that strut over a white page
of snow. The parents and their
children have gone home:
sleds pulled one last time up the hill,
white breath turned a pale blue
before vanishing behind them.

The cold was everywhere
as the crows took the hill, this
open space between a few
scattered trees.

What would the suicides think
after seeing these proud black
pieces of night? Would they
give up, take it back,
put away their guns, their
blades, their pills?

The sky brings on shadows
that lengthen toward the east,
blue and long, and these
birds swirl upward, one
by one, taking refuge
in the arms of the winter trees.

The Weak Man

He isn't much. They placed him in his own
tiny ring away from the main acts and
big lights. High above, in the big top
climes, acrobats dressed like
Greek gods and super heroes
defy gravity and amaze the crowd
with mind-bending spectacle while --
there he is: half in shadow,
a smile against his face,
he'd become a dog beaten so often
that every hand was now an enemy.
His spine bent and rubbery, two pale
arms dangled white at his sides,
ending with ten twitching fingers
unable to make the simplest fist,
while down below, wobbling
hairless and obscene, knees scabbed
from years of crawling.

And while the tight-rope walkers flirt with
the abyss, and the beautiful women stand
proud on the backs of Arabian stallions -- white
teeth grin from flashing red lips, he
kicks at some sawdust, coughs, then
swallows hard. Clumsily, he attemps
to wipe some drool from the corners of his
mouth but fails.

Then the lights go up; it wasn't the first time they'd
forgotten about him -- his act -- they just didn't have time
in between the lion's gaping maw and the elephants

in hoola skirts dancing; between the troupe that
juggled flaming chainsaws and the chimpanzee
dressed out like Evil Knieval jumping five pick-up
trucks on a turbo-powered mini bike.

The people are leaving. The people are gone.

One by one the lights go out.

A jungle cat growls hungry over by the tent
where the animals are kept.

Fifty White Envelopes

during a break
in Thanksgiving
activities
in the basement
the dirty magazines
my cousin showed me
her father collected
after world war two
put away in the musty
cobwebbed trunk
i still remember /
and the stories
of men tortured
by huge and god-like
women, how
those brave men
suffered, how
that yellow
paper felt against
the tips of my fingers,
and later,
in my room
alone

Element of Shame

His name was Larry,
a skinny kid, nervous, odd,
lived with his grandparents
and I lived with mine
one block away. We rode
bikes, climbed trees, killed time
the way twelve-year-old boys
kill time, still I never felt
at ease when I was around him:
there was an element of shame.

The crawlspace beneath
his house always seemed
to have three or four inches
of water reaching out of the darkness.
I couldn't explain the crawlspace.
All I remember is cobwebs --
cobwebs, and the light of a flashlight
falling against nothing.

One evening, I tied Larry
to the catalpa tree in my backyard,
rode off on my bike. I circled
the block. I felt the cool breeze
and listened to the cicadas.

When I returned he was
still there, tied to that tree,
in shadow, crying, fighting away
at the ropes. I fumbled about,
untied the knots. Off he went, home.

Bigfoot, My Love

From the black forest Bigfoot cries
out to me, ever-expanding ripples
of sadness, a wall almost solid
with sorrow. I cover my ears and that
doesn't help; the blood-red moon winces
from its hole in the sky -- this plea,
this gargantuan lover's plea avalanching
through all the arteries of our ancient
nightscape -- stars hold their breath,
the wind stops blowing; leaves hang
in silence. Bigfoot doesn't want to die
any more than we do!

But I am lost. I listen to this song
of a creature that never really existed,
a sound coming from a place located
only in dreams and poems. I listen until
the breeze resumes its momentum,
and these stars go tumbling on across the night.

Another Recipe

"take a sad song and make it better"

They have peeled back
the horrible onions & slash
into the garlic's thin flesh, swig
of beer as the blade goes down,
jack-off zucchini & toss olive oil into
the heating skillet, the knife slides
sideways into a carrot, smash the garlic
free of skin, turn it all over, smile into
the mirror, then, very carefully, take the
dish of chicken parts & plop it all
into the heat, another beer, feed
yourself, let it happen. The forks have
all been hidden. What a dismal time.
Too much. Write a letter about
how I should fight to live, fight
this life. Or something. New York
wanted to kill me. But I thought
it would. No surprise. "Hey Jude,"
they all said, "Judy, Judy, Judy, Judy, Judy --
Na na na na. Hey --" Yes, & dinner
is now served.

This Transitional Life

Late December afternoon, listening
to James Brown sing Christmas songs,
for no reason I walk to the window
and pull open the blinds: down in the
parking lot of the building next door
a hearse sits, and four people:
two women, two men in long, dark coats,
are discussing something. Soon they
go inside, in a matter of minutes
emerging with a gurney, a grey
sheet covers everything, shrouds the
huge gut, the feet, the face, and with
some effort they guide the contraption
through the doorway and down
three steps into the lot. The woman
wearing the light blue jeans and
sweat shirt keeps coughing, keeps
bending over and covering her mouth.
The other three don't seem bothered,
they wait patiently as she walks off,
gags, waves her hands about in the air.
Soon, though, they lift what is
left into the car. One man gets in and
braces himself behind the wheel,
the other one goes back inside with
the two women. James has stopped
singing five minutes ago. That's when
I notice, out of the corner of my eye,
the squirrel on a power line marching off
toward an over-flowing dumpster.

The Old Man's Coat

I remember: it was long and dark, not black,
a little brown maybe thrown in, with
subtle shades of red criss-crossing through.
It made me think of Bogart, of course,
and gat-packing gangsters in black and white
alleys, up against the wall clutching at
their entrance wounds as if love had made
them suddenly aware, aware of their
own bodies for the first time; but it wasn't
love and it wasn't death and it wasn't
the mailman or the milkman. It was only
the hiss of night coming, shoe leather on
brick streets wet with rain, of deep focus --
of film sliding brittle through light, frame after
frame. I took it: one sleeve at a time.

The End Of The Day

She is there, next to
me, what can you do? Drink
it down, live it up. I study her
vague features through this
room's half-light. She is always
different, changes minute to minute.
Blue eyes, brown eyes, green.

Live the end of the day up. Let the
candle burn. I blink and this world has
changed. One day you will burn.
In the next room, the one that was
never built, a child sleeps
through its nothingness, safe in
a bed of air. Listen to the voices
coming to you from across
that room. We will do things together:
we will go to the park
on Sundays, eat dinner together
at our dining-room table, discussing
the day, the day that never happened.
You and I caught between two extremes.

After all, I am the drunken man with a baby
on his lap. I tell the baby:
this is the steering wheel, now drive.
My foot falls against the gas. Let's go.

Then I wake up, next to her,
and she looks at me with her eyes:
her blue eyes, her brown eyes, her green.

There Are Dreams

There are dreams that come and go and leave no trace.
Man is animal, man is beast. We shiver in the night when
dreams come and we can't believe our thoughts
-- a palace has turned into a slum. Simon

& Garfunkle are looking for America now in the long
dream that skims the surface of a quiet pond just off this
Missouri backroad; I am there with a girl I once thought
I loved -- swimming in the muddy water, holding her
as we drifted, our faces full of sun, just drifting, that's all.

The Haunted House

And this is the haunted house you
love so much inside you full of
cold chills misty visions low against
the ground   love because love in the only
word stuffed with the musings of spiders
here love is the full yellow moon hung
in the cloudless Autumn night   a flat
round light on the slow dissolve
into day   you feel your way   thrills
shivers   you walk through the rusty
iron gate   the owl goes hoot hoot hoot
you can feel each rock beneath your shoes
hair rises up on the neck   the black cat
arches its back from the top of the picket
fence   aerosol hiss   the wind swoops
down rattles through leaves   reminds
you of nothing as mad laughter bounces
down from that window candle-lit furthest
up lonely attic room   maniacal guttural
nothing is funny   far from funny
but the laughter continues   the black
cat devours its shadow and the wind
blows out the candle and all you have
then is the cold dark touching every inch
of you covered in the deep light
possessed by the Other   all the Others
that drag log chains over rough attic
wood moaning through eternity's veil
they have emerged the opposite of light
saturated by distance   forgotten
they have no hands to hold

only time's acrid vibrato pushing forth
you   you are only flesh   they are
timeless in a timeless place   you
go into the house   tiny voices leap
into air   out of every crack
the untranslatable murmur   snap
in the air   the only light is the full moon
and we speak of love because this is what
we simply must do

For Lennon

You and Nilsson burning down the town,
Yoko-less, boys again, drunk, stoned -- kicked out
of every bar for childish pranks, pure
life rolling through the night until you came
around, I guess, to the hangover, and for
the last time you said "good-bye" to the wild
side; turned it all over to the Ono
love of your life and the kids -- then came
the last few songs, the last music -- the music
of a well-placed bullet pushed your way
by a man that had found himself a stranger
in his own life. Outside, beneath the shadow
of that brownstone, you folded into legend.

Attempted Suicide

This is, after all, some place else we're going.
Oblivion leaks through the day-light fabric, arranges
pathetic shadows for our eyes. I could sit here at
this desk forever and think of nothing else.
I'd allow the street light entrance through these
parted blinds; obscenities forming, never articulated.
There is so much water in the world, oceans and
oceans of water. Streams and streams of it. We should

be fishing and drinking beer, fishing and naked on
the bank of that unforgettable river where fish speak
words for love and birds dive down to them, dip into
the swirling foam, and rise up again into the noon
sun that will never stop shining, lost to those flying
throats that swoop and bank and split off as shards of
movement, splinters of blue, yellow, red. You did not

plan this, but you made it happen: these words
arranged on paper. Once, maybe, I wanted to return
to that place, but I never did, only approaching it in
the freedom of a dream, disguised as a leopard.

The sun was beginning to disappear into the evening
when you drove into the Liberty Park lagoon. A few men
nearby tried to help as the car floated there, sinking.

You slapped one of them, rolled up the window, locked
the doors, your seat belt holding you tight. Finally, two
policemen arrived, pulled you from that murky place.

As a child I skipped around this man-made lagoon, kicked

my way into the blue on the park's swing sets -- I have
no clear picture now. You told one of the rescuers
he had no right to do what he was doing. I wasn't there,
but I could hear the water splashing, the grind of traffic
three blocks away, and the voices of cicadas sprouting
from almost every tree in that small, small town.

The Fireplace

He was in a room. He was trying to get
out. Where was the door? There was no

door. Where was the window? There was
no window. Where was the emergency exit?

There was no emergency exit. Where was
the secret passage-way in the fireplace?

There was no secret passage-way. There was
no fireplace. There were four walls, a ceiling,

& a floor. He knocked on each of the four
walls with his knuckles the way you would knock

on a door. He tried to reach the ceiling,
but it was too high to reach. He jumped up

& down, stomping on the floor the way an
angry child might do when throwing a tantrum.

He became very tired & fell down & the
hand landed on something cold. It was a

key. He picked up the key & looked at it,
smiling, & was overwhelmed with

happiness. He put the key into the safety
of a pocket; tears staining his face.

Rimbaud's Mother

She pauses in the doorway, searching this
green world, the horizon, her clear eyes set

deep in a private place scanning every inch
of air for a sign -- "Arthur, Arthur! It

is time for supper" -- she holds twisted in
her hands an apron splashed with the blood of

a butchered chicken, the scent of wet grass
constructs a luminous cathedral, a blessing

to all the animals of the field and the
sky -- "Arthur! Where have you gone?

I know where you've gone. Run away again
to that city of soot and grime. That place
of flooded gutters you call Poetry."

October Poem

for Randy Bowlin

He leans back in the red leather booth of
the Chinese buffet, the last plate before
him, laced with bean sprouts, crumbs from
crab rangoon, the fortune cookie still wrapped
in its see-through plastic. He studies
the knife that he didn't use. -- These places
never give you knives -- he thinks. Then the sound --
thudding -- a pulsing -- the windows rattle
mildly, and a car filled with teenagers
cruises by, music turned up until the only
sound is the bass sound thudding, thudding.
It is Autumn and leaves attack sidewalks,
blazing reds, dried and cracked, edge into traffic.
He fingers the cookie; closes his eyes.

Theory & Oblivion In The Writing
Of Contemporary Poetry

for Robert C. Jones

Someone is down by the river
on his knees blessing the rocks
one by one. Farther away,
downstream and up the bluff, old men spit
and roll cigarettes behind
the Quick Shop store in the drizzle.
They are good at it.

I was told years ago that
you needed focus to justify
the flight of birds, to translate
the human spirit as it flaps about
beautiful or lame.

I believe it might be old black
and white Charlie Chan, like
Sunday afternoon television when
I was thirteen, fourteen, fifteen --
yes, there he is squinting
patiently into this generic geology,
in search of the most important
clue of all, the clue that breaks the case.

The ancient highway out front
pulls faceless cars into town,
sending them cleanly out
the other end, all of it, the speed,
the motion, all accompanied
by the invisible swoop
of frantic wings.

There Is A Question

There is a question circling out there somewhere, cut off
from this life I pretend to live. There is an answer, too,
swimming in the sea, rolling in the waves, diving away
from the light. The words to sum up the totality -- those
words ran wild over the plains, they seek the woodlands,
the deep brush, maybe even a cave.

I watched all the nature shows when I was a kid. Men
struggled in marshy ponds wrapped in the endless
vitality of a frightened boa constrictor; life and death
on the TV screen in the shadowless African sun. Birds
the color of the fourth of July sprayed into the wavy air.
The buzzards sat looking on just outside the camera's eye.

From The Dead End Tavern (Spokane, WA)

to Ted & Ted's dad

When people come here, they come alone; walk
inside to get away from the cold rain,
shake their wet selves and use both hands smoothing
back their hair -- feeling the dirty water
snake down tired necks. No one is shooting pool,
and only a few lean against the bar.
It's Sunday, and it's a little after
eight in the morning. The only thing on
tap is Old Milwaukee, eighty cents for
a glass. The glass is always dirty, some
lipstick smudge clinging ghostly to its rim;
but no one seems to mind this, it only
makes sense -- look around, buddy, only ghosts
here. This is the end, this is the dead end.

lullaby

1.

Pushed, pulled out of that believing place, cleaned off,
made to cough, breathe, eyes still squinted against
the light of day, the bald medical light
exposing each tiny flaw, sounds come out
with slime and puke and coughs that seem to say
"please please please I don't want this change right now"
no, to go from that embryonic world,
a paradise of dark fluid, cradled
in the soft and murky cave of womb-flesh,
solemn heaven where the drift of things asks
no questions, asleep and awake are much
the same -- and the light -- what light there is, is

2.

muted, distant -- undulating colors
without boundaries, and is it all blind
anyway? No memory here, just second-
hand knowledge, stuff found in books, television,
this naked screaming thing, a creation
of sperm and egg and fuck-lust, lust for life,
clawing and biting -- orgasm plunge deep
into the empty wet void, life on top
of life, juices intermingle, science
whispers into history's ear: present,
past, future -- a long tongue, closes off the
opening -- you are out, ready or not.

3.

That was nineteen March nineteensixtyone,
mother'd been watching wrestling on tv
with her father, that is when the water
broke, that is when the hospital trip was
made, and her legs spread wide to allow my
entrance/exit -- my birth, my cleansing bath
in new water, wrapped in blankets, given
to my mother to hold, finally sleep
comes, sleep without symbols and without dreams,
lost in an abstract landscape, protected from
the teeth of sharks, claws of jungle cats
protected from these words men sometimes use.

4.

Out of the hospital, then, and home: home,
twentytwo-eleven South Harrison,
in the town of Sedalia, Missouri --
wrapped in warm blankets against chilled March winds,
there, now, to live with mother, grandmother,
and grandfather. Peggy, Pearl, and John -- "this is
it" -- I would've said if I could've said
anything -- but all I did was suck my hand,
and sleep, and eat, and the other thing -- and
day was night and night was day, no time
filled my head with worry, my murmurs filled
the lives of Peggy, Pearl, and John. Yes. Yes.

5.

Outside at night the blue wind blows into
another world. The birds and leaves go round
and round, dancing circles in the air: then
all is lost in this middle of chaos,
this sound, this fury -- imagination
fills the blood and eyes closed tight see inside
out until, at last, there is no worry.
This is a lullaby. The bridges fall
into the drowsy river washed away
down-stream, Negro songs follow it all down.
Nothing really ever gets done in this
place where unnamed flowers anoint the air.

6.

Time of resting, time of mumbling voices
warm voice music, bathed, powdered, given love:
why? Why not? What is love? Beautiful thing,
that life, in a crib as the sun goes down,
spilling gold in through the western window,
all things: the color of antiquity --
while in the kitchen grandmother sings old
tunes popular during world war two, stirs
a pot of something, suppertime soon for
the ones with teeth; the house fills up with warmth
as the old floor furnace rattles, kicks on:
all working together to achieve this

7.

moment retrieved from thin air, a rabbit
pulled from a hat: a magic trick, shadow
box desire to return to a place
called home, beyond home, where music boxes
evoke various strategies, consult
democratic cosmologies, open
pale doors infused with distance and allow
the deep bawling inside to spill out where
melancholy evening waits, this birth
of something like music, a hunger for
action that raises the roof, sets things in
motion. You can only nap for so long.

8.

I know you are not lonely, you're almost
nothing, a bundle of nothing in the
gurgling crib, covered snug and warm by a
blue baby blanket. The air above you
sighs its emptiness down to your tiny
ears -- but that is where the signal begins
to die. Two blue eyes blink, two tiny fists
shake for no reason, white and chubby, bang
into the little nose, chin, and can hurt,
and it does, but you don't stop until the
wind blows through the window, splitting in two
faded curtains with the scent of lilac.

9.

Breastfeeding didn't work for my mother
so it was the bottle that I suckled,
the formula filled my tummy with its
formulaic nurtrition. I don't know --
could this've been a problem? Still, how nice an
early nipple, warm and wet at my face,
would've been. But, anyway, she did smoke
and no doubt nursed certain alcoholic
drinks that would not have been so good for me.
There is a photo of my grandfather
and me -- he holds a bottle to my mouth.
So little I am there with him, plastic

10.

in lips. He has just come home from his job
at the railroad shops. He wears a baseball
cap, dirty, and bent at the bill, his hands
are cracked and weathered, they hold me with care.
There are also photos of my mother
and me, but for some reason I am not
as touched by them as I am the one with
him, John Preisendorf. His gray hair, his clear
eyes that look off past the camera's eye:
what is he thinking? Eyes that have seen two
world wars unfold; but always the wrong age,
always a little bit too young or old.

11.

David Bowie told us to "run for the
shadows" -- what did he mean? I think I know,
I think I knew then. The shadows were where
the strange and interesting things happened.
At night they'd hang on the wall by windows,
across from windows, and outside almost
everything seemed as if it were shade,
shadow -- silouette. Black and black and black --
with quick stabs of street-light punctuating
a mysterious landscape of absence :
all of this was so endless, cut loose from
life, a broad expanse of golden years.

12.

Crybaby'd cry whenever a stranger
came to visit, he'd let out a howl of
enormous proportion, and the dog that
I believe I forgot to mention, would
begin to howl -- little Cindy; we'd
put an end to polite conversation.
After a while I guess the crying stopped.
That is, until little Cindy stole toys
thrown at her -- what fun! -- and under the couch
she'd cringe and bare her small, white teeth until
some one would retrieve the object, give it
back to the wailing little child, me, Paul.

13.

Things hang, things dangle, jiggle from above
and rotate, all as funny as can be.
Shapes come into view and just as swiftly
disappear. Blurred edges provide mixture,
a work of art is being created,
continuous work in progress, constant
amazement, shifting of forms with only
the vaguest hint of an idea, plan,
or strategy behind any of it.
And these dust motes that dance in evening
sunlight, fractured pieces of space, eyes watch
them as they unfold their plotless story.

14.

After awhile, it's crawling and walking,
or rather trying to walk, hold the hand,
one foot in front of the other, in that
way we'll find ourselves in another
place much different from this one we're in
now. Teeter-totter movements, back and forth,
the mad rush forward, from this place to that
plateau, that hill's peak, sunny or cloudy,
until there is only one way and that
way is up -- up where stars kill time, twinkling;
and to break through this high black firmament --
there must be something past all the nothing.

15.

In front of the TV in the living
room on my plastic toilet; learned to use
the potty there as cowboys fought redskins,
as Superman flew faster than bullets --
there I'd squat and wait for something to come
out of my butt. So many mysteries!
What kind of life was playing out beneath
the surface of that glass? Giant apes grabbed
women from the safety of bedrooms,
took them to the top of the world. This was love,
too. From my tiny throne I surveyed the
world's fantastic, dramatic unfolding.

16.

O the buzzing bee glow summer hill romp
early morning steamy grass and dew shines
feet baby-naked toes clutch the stiff blades
and dirt beneath is a little cooler --
yes, and in a lawn chair nearby mother
reads romance novel in the patio's
shade. This is the life. Wobbling and crawling --
follow the butterfly's zigzag frolic
into the neighbor's yard; mother is lost
in her book -- you, you discover the world
unknown, you stumble, fall -- you cut your leg,
scream for mother in that far other place.

17.

That one Christmas, bit into the small glass
ornament, silver flakes filled my mouth,
and a scream came bursting forth; every
one came running -- made me spit, shined flashlight
down my throat until they were certain they'd
gotten all of it out. And there was that
time: on the iron grill of the furnace, two
knees collided one winter. You could hear me
for blocks, they said. Mom smeared on some kind of
ointment and all was well. What are these strange
admonitions of mortality that
are paracelled out to us on winter nights?

18.

Down the long street where huge grasshoppers hop,
and beneath a sky filled with eagles that
like to eat little boys, snag them, take them
off to a place in the clouds high above
the land below where stupid cows count their
toes and munch on cud. Down the longest day
there ever was, full of sunshine and love.
Down the gravel road to the old bridge that
whispers to us from the other side, tells
stories from a place before time began
to unravel, and in the process, we
sprang into the world, holding on for life.

19.

When was it that I was given that bear?
The brown little Teddy Bear; and we called
him Teddy, and Teddy would sleep with me
and wake with me; and in dreams we'd go
on picnics in the tall, dark woods, dance to
a primeval tune that oozed up from roots
and mud, filled our bones with joy until down
we'd fall onto the thick green grass, out of
breath, the whole world spinning out of control.
This was a time of morning mist and song --
and at dusk fog came to those low places
where Teddy Bear and I would run and hide :

20.

in between trees we'd sit in that stillness
of a great world that I knew little of,
our singular silence held each moment
compressed in private perfection, nothing
could sever our vast equalibrium,
we embraced the sky painted over with
stars, allowed the mighty thing to tower
above both our ragged heads -- worshipful
eyes peering into an infinite place
where numbers boil in a witch's cauldron.
Teddy, what next, after this place, this home,
where dreams alone nurture the hope we share?

21.

I will create a photo now because
none, to my knowledge, exists : There we are,
in that white Chevy, and the day is hot,
or so it seems, windows rolled down,
bright light covers the car's interior --
Grandfather at the wheel, my grandmother
at his side -- their two stoic faces lost
in thought, watching the road ahead.
I am in the back seat with my mother.
How old am I? I don't know. She smiles down
at me as if it were a great distance --
but it isn't, it is not far at all.

Two

Other Dimensional Beings

> "this isn't science fiction
> anymore -- it's science."
>   -guy on a late night radio show

All day long wires infiltrate
the ground   walking is a dangerous
adventure   we could disappear
come back as another entity
above the pyramid   floating
comatose in a diagram of sky
all teeth gone cows run away
in fear   this is the angelic language
spoken by those gray men
those travelers through space
and time   all is embraced
within the confines of our cosmic
arena   the words for peace
and harmony go unspoken   you'd
never believe me if I told you
how it is   many lives passed
through the axis of my stance
when I saw that moon last night
and my feet were electrified
this was electricity   each alien
molecule holding court in
the unfolding universe that is
me

On Being Asked Again For Something By Someone I Didn't Know

(From Jackson Square, New Orleans)

I don't have anthing   I don't I don't I don't
have what you want or need I don't have
a coherent knowledge of history   I don't like
to get out of bed in the morning but I do
and I wish I knew why but I don't   I don't
have what it takes but I take what I see
what I think it will take to allow the being
that I am to continue in the hours through
the hours breathing up the time that holds
my feet against this pavement this needy
thing called Paul with my eyes and hands
and stomach I wish I could understand
but I can't understand anything so I write
this message in the light of my confession
of lack and when I'm finished I will rip this
page out and roll it up find a bottle -- insert --
cork tightly   it will be dedicated to all those
who are driven to ask strangers for some-
thing they do not have and it is dedicated
to strangers who have nothing   and off
the bottle will go   taken out back to the
shallow muddy pond where cows go to
drink   the bottle will bob into the little
waves catching the sun's midday glare
not wanting to leave me when I give
the offering a push   but it does
finally it does

Disturbing Messages

Again they speak of Bigfoot's ghostly presence,
words coming out of this late night talk show

Purity is a difficult thing to evaluate

Nebulous   random   cosmicabominable

The cold is not the same as it was back then
sunshine entered my body in a different way

The woods were filled with screams
and love and disturbing messages

The cave went in deep, and dropping,
as it did, moaned the way the dying moan

Later it is time to simply pause,
drink in the light that seeps down

the light that can't, that light that will
never, the light that tastes like blood

on snow or mother's milk in a paper cup

Heavenly Hill

Are you all right? he says.

I am the ghost-teacher

I am the historian

I wlll be on the corner over there

with all the secrets from the past

All right?   Are you all right?

I can't stand up very long like this

I'm old   I will be over there   on the corner

I know this city   I know all the secrets

Look   Look   I have cancer   Look

at my arms   I'm 74   I need to sit down

I will be there   just over there   on the corner

Dear Mr. Benton:

What you are doing is a mistake --
Leaving here for there will not work,
you will be alone as alone can be --
your eyes glued shut by darkness will not see --

Those people, you don't know, will eat you whole,
will use your bones in their midnight ritual --
this world of mouths, it talks behind your back,
the doll in the drawer with your name speaks --
        "heart-attack" --

So please don't go, I can't be
responsible now -- just know that I have
been there -- lost there -- in that snow

The Bitter Man

growled, and when standing -- stood alone: eyes've
become hard, and hands that hang from the end of
sleeves are restless; tough skin rubbing together,
long fingers push through hair -- looks as if there
is a search ongoing for a piece dislocated,
a misplaced artifact of some consequence. No one
talks to him now. What's-passed-is-past lingers --

the permanence that is resolve congeals inside bone,
inside heart; and as evening spreads out its wide,
dark blanket -- he will go walking, and his foot-steps,
each upon each of them, construct their own proposal
against the seasons -- and he has become fearful of
those twilight dogs always up ahead, their
leashes beautiful in the street-light light,
their teeth exposed, white.

Sonnet (Bicycling Home After Work)

Home home going home Chartres street along
the Mississippi invisible on
the concrete otherside the levee over
there as I move with the night and this thump
of wheel of movement car after car long
notes punctuated mournful in wave and
light bring home close with each rotation
the song of all this having no title
it is all just free   there in a real place
beyond streetlights as the heavy giant
sways back and forth dark motion metallic
rattle   the unseen pulls this animal
slowly past me I'm gliding along face
faces the wind swaying home home homeward.

Popcorn

I began. Out. And continue. There you go.
You go in and you go out. Another six
minutes. Could be another life. Quick
the winter comes. Then it goes. Is always,
kind of, there. Put on the hat, take it
off. Sky blue sky passes over. I remember
the rose I gave you one day. 25 years
is gone. The leaf falls from the tree
and decorates the yard. Another log
graces the fireplace. When the world began
was it summer? Was it spring? What
was the first season? I like popcorn
with real butter on it. Then they
invented the calendar and one day passed
after the other. I found you in the
mirror. It was smashed.
The middle of the road. Cars kept
coming. I tried to pick up the
pieces.

The Nail

The nail is in the street, sharp

end up, up to all

possibility.   You see it,

gray on gray, the morning

light, the blue sky threatens

to overwhelm -- the word

for "you" is forgotten,

the place called home isn't --

you could be walking, crawling,

riding a bicycle, driving

a car -- it would all be the

same.   The nail in the morning

street cannot go unnoticed.

To Take It There

for D. S.

He wanted to take it there -- that was the day &
he was alive & the room was full of light --
one song after the other -- he wanted it -- he
needed it -- the collision of sound as the

afternoon began its fading -- neighbors growing
annoyed -- take it there -- he wanted to be taken
there -- pull the gigantic essence into
focus -- he needed it more than he needed

life -- when it came to life there was a missing
link -- life just wasn't enough -- in the fading
into the evening -- & he turned up the volume --
song after song - each song I suggested -- they

just weren't doing it -- taking him to that place he
needed to go -- he began naming off songs &
I began to find those songs but when I played
them -- each song -- turning up the volume -- a look

would come over his face -- he squinted his eyes
tightly closed -- it wasn't happening -- nothing was
doing it -- if it had been twenty years ago he would
have ripped off his shirt & ran out the door &

into the street -- breaking bottles dancing barefoot
on the fine sharp glass -- but it wasn't twenty years
ago -- it was that afternoon -- & it wasn't working --
he couldn't get there -- to that place -- & his eyes
closed so tight.

Electronic Telepathy

The way is pure. If you want to find
a way out. This is all that I really believe: You
need to forget many things. Say: I forget
and I forgive. Take one of those leaflets they
hand out on the street and read it then throw
it away. Forget. Forgive. But this isn't
new, nothing new here. Look your loved
one in the face and decide what you need to
do. Do you love your loved one? The time we
have trickles away, you know. Stare into the
man's eyes. The man you don't know that happens

to be walking down the same sidewalk as you --
he is going in the opposite direction. He is going
south and you are going north. You have said
many things in your life so far. Many words
have passed between your lips, flopped out
into the air, made music, sang the song. The
world is chaotic inside its randomness. The radio
station delivers me the color of a faraway distance now --
tells me night is becoming morning -- tells me all kinds
of things -- repeats the word until the word
begins to make just enough sense.

Drinks Are Free

The words of love   I don't know
lost the dictionary too many days
back   the memory shrinks
I don't know my own name
it isn't my name
it is your name

along the night street we disappear
death is the simplest of obligations --
I don't want to dwell there now,
salvation boils my blood

Yeats is behind the bar
drinks are free
men are kissing dogs out
in the raw noon street
they have embraced the truest impulse

I can't imagine anything better.

Hello, There Is No Hope

Goodbye.   What do you want?   It doesn't
matter too much what you want.

I love you.   That doesn't matter either.
The sky is blue & the sun is
high above & potent.   The moon
brings the tide to an organic
climax.

We have all lied to you, but we
didn't mean it.   There was no malice:
it was just something that broke --
waved onto this dishevelled beach,
almost dawn -- an evolutionary
convergence, split atoms &
plastic history.

If you think, if you believe
I meant any harm, you
are wrong.   The hand was blind.
The mouth said hello &
the other mouth said goodbye.

Found Poem

"Paul Benton,

Look forward to seeing
you when it's
advisable. I will
bring you a free
Planner and go over
our properties, which
are the best in
the city. Metairie
Cemetary is a National
Historic place
one of the top ten
cemetaries in
the World. Lake Lawn
is next door."

signed:
D.N.

Bigfoot In The Mojave

This could never happen then -- only now --
and you were wrong enough because

man is weak and man is ill, always
conceding to the plague that falls

that inserts its own sickness into
the flow   the blood   tarantula bite

my god   and midnight pulls up
its own nightmare   takes flight

toward the last obscurity   pulling out
ancient blood rivers from unknown

flesh with no voice   no talking at all --
a sad dead face allows itself

exposure   in the middle   where
it is empty and big and complete.

Yesterday The Fortune Teller Was Crying

The snake waits by the door.
You have lost your keys again
and it starts to rain.
Yesterday, or the day before,

it was different. But how
different it was I can't say --
won't say -- you will find the key
that takes you into where you'll stay --

everyone has seen this future.
Hide the handkerchief. Piss, piss
over there by the trash can, kiss
the hand that feels the pain. Endure.

XXX

to Davey Jones, Daydream Believer

They tell you one thing and then another
thing

They tell you that they've loved you
then they say No they haven't loved you

it all gets rather mixed up

let it go

you walk down the street   the street is
pure and true   nothing better

you were wrong too   you said love and
then you didn't mean it   you stopped

meaning it   the voices of two angry people
come out of a window
fill up the street   the world

this is impossibly obvious   tell me
what I need to know so I can
make it all

better

Lost (on Decatur Street)

The morning is cruel
Where did we go?
You need to go
Time will take you
Man is a fool

This is the place
Harmonic atonal
The meaning is struggle
Where is the devil?
Lost out in space

The rat finds the river
I find my self
Surfers surf
No one is safe
Take from the giver

The car hits the dog
A firecracker sound
The dog dances around
Good as dead
Looking for God

God doesn't exist
This street is a wide one
A girl screams at the sun
See the little dog run
I think I need to rest

That Wide, Open Feeling

Gone almost as soon as it appears, slicing
into the daily routine, there is a
parting, a pulling apart of the internal
fabric that in no way can be located
with x-rays or probing fingers --
that wide, open feeling looks you
in the face from its own perfect
dimension and you look back,
no choice, into what you believe
are the most beautiful eyes you have
ever seen.

Then you don't know
who you are and it doesn't matter
because one day will become
one night and the dark and the light
look the same.   The sounds in the
street blend and fall and rise.
That feeling -- crowded, empty as
a clock, all motion pulling against
whatever there is to pull against --
wide open, brilliant, subliminal.

These two goldfish, here now,
in their little backyard pond,
in the shade of the green bush,
bees circling about in the air,
these fish are hungry, they have
not been fed.

Bourbon Street, After Work

He wanted something. He had a dollar
bill in his hand and night was on his face.
The door opened: and there he was, and his
eyes were white -- he said, "Here, give me something."
I was taking out the trash; it was one
in the morning. I could see his eyes and
when he spoke I thought I could see his teeth.
"What?" "I'm hungry. Give me something." "I don't
have anything. I'm sorry." He moved closer,
held onto the side of the door. "Give me
something." I pulled the door shut. He seemed to
dissolve. There was the hand with the dollar,
then there wasn't anything at all.

The Lazy Man
(overheard at the Sugar Park Tavern)

After three wives and four kids and
a job that I hated, all of those endless
days that added up to make each
of those hollow years of my life --
after that, after more than that --
I decided to only do what I wanted
to do. I hung it up. Six months
went by and I didn't leave my
little apartment. Each one of those
days seemed to me like money in the bank.
Pure and true and bullshit-free.
I watched the paint peel, I watched
the sink fill up with dishes,
I watched the sun come up and I
watched the sun go down, and at night
I got drunk and stoned with
the moon: that lonely looking thing
punctuating my dark landscape.

I was the lazy man now and I had
all my food delivered, beer delivered --
I'd look out the window, the big one
looking out on the nice little street
and there the cars went back and forth
and the people on bicycles and the
people walking. The occasional
wheelchair wobbled onward beneath
leafy shadows. I observed all this human
drama unfolding and counted myself
lucky to be where I was: behind that door,

behind that glass, alone in that good space.

Finally, one day around noon, I made
my way back out into the new world. I stood
under a tree and listened to sounds
the breeze made in my ears. I felt like
a god that wasn't responsible for the things
it'd created. Then I went back in and
called one of my kids. We talked for a
little while then they asked if they could
have some money. I hung up. I went
down the street to the Sugar Park tavern
and had several beers. It was a good time
that went on for most of the night.

In fact, that was some years ago now --
and I'm still here, if not here, then some
where else, but one thing is for certain
I don't do anything I don't want to do,
and you're sure as hell not going to find me
some place I don't want to be.

The Ice Cream Man Is Burning

The place is on fire
the entire place
flames devour holy man
and infidel alike
the young girls
unblemished, lurch
down the street
human torch-light
uncorrupted, screams
buzzsaw into smoke
pigeons dissolve into
feathery ash.

I have found the river
and watch from a distance
that mimics surgery
gone wrong. People
run toward me,
begging for just
a little more --
more life, more love
more impossibility.
I side-step and they
splash into the moving water
and are carried away.

Then I see him.
The ice cream man.
Here he comes,
his flame is white
and he is laughing,

he is crying, his body
bulges, cracks.
There is something
different here,
I think to myself
as I watch him go in
and down with the rest.

The Magical

The breeze   the light   the warmth
the grass   the shadows   the paper
the lines around everything   the
leaves   the cigarette butts   the tourists
the mothers   the sons   the sleeping
cats   the waving American flag
the beat drummed   the electric guitar
the mule wagons   the laughter   the thoughts
that people have   the evening approaches
the river unseen   the singing voice
the birds at the drinking fountain
the dog   the leash   the hands we
hold   the bridge that spans   the flute
the rose   the clock made out of iron
the magical adjustment of this situation

You Have Won

How we go on how do we go on how we
do go on and it isn't a dance it isn't
a crawl maybe it is pulling teeth but
not as factual or being without medication
and needing medication
trying to destroy repetition but still
inside the heart beats its way through
the day it beats the dream beats sleep
awake horizontal journey alive in black
silence no one can know much for long
beneath the tree sun going from sky
not moving become essential closed up
as a whisper all the mail is junk mail
you have won you are a winner the prize
is yours and the whisper is your voice
the sky becoming light blue violet pale
pale the sky is a drifting arrangement
the breath of a whisper two crows fly
through it

Shoes

She wanted the shoes.
I went and found and brought her the shoes.
She smiled and was happy. Young and sexy and happy.
She planned on making money with the shoes. They
would bring things to her that would make life good.
The shoes cost $59.99 plus tax and off she went out
the door and into the evening.

In an hour she was back. One of the shoes
had broken, the strap came undone,
the stitch job gave way. I went into the backroom
and tried to find her a replacement. Size 7. There were
no size 7's. I came back to tell her there were none
left in that size. "Well, what about this one," she
had a shoe in her hand, showing it to me. I took the
shoe, went back, looked. No. I returned with a similar
shoe in a size 7-- trying to placate her. She looked at
it with a dismal expression on her pretty face.
"OK I'll take them but I don't like it."
"I'm sorry," I said, "I'm sorry."
She grabbed the shoes, exchanged them at a loss.

An hour passed and I was folding shirts in the back
of the store when I noticed by the front door
one of my co-workers talking to someone,
patting them on the back, their back was heaving --
they were crying.

It was her again. In two minutes she was gone.
Then I got the story: the shoes, she hated the shoes,
and at some point, she realized her phone was missing--

she'd lost her phone -- and she didn't know anyone --
she was from Mississippi and she was alone.
The night had grown darker. Things weren't going
the way she'd envisioned them. What would happen
next? But she was gone now, and I went back to
folding those goddamn T-shirts.

The Bee

The honey bee. There it goes. Like
everything, I guess, flying away on an
April breeze. When I was four or five
I was walking barefoot, nearly naked,
across the lawn and it was early morning,
or mid-morning, or almost afternoon.
The sun was formidable and strong up in
that unknowable blue ocean of sky.
I was there, beneath it all, wobbling
in the green, observing the way
light falls on grass -- the way trees
grow out of shadow. And then
the pain, the foot that was my foot,
my eyes filled with tears when I saw
the little bee, fuzzy and squirming,
bouncing among those green blades.
I ran home, tears and screams, the
shadows and the trees, the blue of the
sky and the bee in its death and everything
lost out there on that April breeze.

Valentino

for Bob Carter

You were gone before anyone
arrived
                just not really
here, just elsewhere
                down the beach
                        in the dunes

playing in the mountains
                        your pants around your ankles
a lion killing sheep
                there was no escape

we sat up all night
                        discussing philosophy
literature   that art stuff
around sun-up we'd start
to pass out

        then sleep would take us
for a few hours
maybe until noon
                        or a little after

and then   goddamn   it would start
                                all over
again

how sweet it all seemed   how
cool the shade was
from those trees

Death Of Numbers

The mathematician divides his time
between thought and thoughlessness,
this life lived out just far enough
away from one tumultuous ball of
flame and energy. He paces the
sterile floor, agonizing over one equation
after the other.

How long has it been
since his head fell into the comfort
of a pillow? He no longer remembers
the last time he saw the ocean,
the waves -- counting each one as it slapped
flat onto the beach -- the endless process
called time.

He discovers a mistake and quickly erases it.

Orson Welles in 'Touch of Evil'

He flops, an old carp
in a sea of shadow

he brought me
a gift, a sugar skull.

Overgrown, he
was, in every way:

"I'm belonging,"
he said in a letter,

"to the last place
in a way that's first."

Almost dead in
that black river

separating two
countries, bullet

hole, bullet hole
"How are you

today?" he
wrote. Almost

dead now, slumped
back in the

fetid mix

slowly pulling

him down, just
another piece

of man-kind, --
the gift melts

in my pocket

On The East Bank Of The Mississippi River, New Orleans

They come here to drown they don't know
it but they come here they come here to
drown even if it isn't certain and they
don't know what they are doing
they come here to this place this time
to drown in a way that no one understands
but they understand and they have come
here to drown in a way that no one can
understand in the way that those who
come to drown and in drowning they
will come to understand that what they
have done is a coming and a going and a
finding of a place to come to and drown
in a place of places that understands
as much about drowning as any place
you want to know

Epitaph

"the epitaph is the aftermath" -- Tom Waits

All of it is forgotten.   What I did.
The mouth could be saying,
"What happened?"   The coca-cola
truck turns right at the corner.
Certain events transpired, lines
were crossed. The faucet that was
twisted on was twisted off.
Thunder always seemed to be
in the distance. The tourist
stumbled because he had not
walked these streets.   Heaven is
the streets, hell is the streets,
being afraid to move, being
asleep, being too drunk to see
the faces coming at you.
Listening to the thunder beneath
a tree that could pass for the
tree in the first garden. The bell
behind me rings down the time;
a helicopter transgresses its way
north.   On this piece of paper
a large yellow-faced fly lands,
rubbing its paws together.

The Day I Killed Bigfoot

The day before yesterday, I think, or
the day before that, I'm not sure if the
date matters now; it was one of those days
in that long string of days that brings alive
each story -- but, anyway I was out
there, and the wind was blowing from what seemed
like every direction at once. What
am I doing?   What song was I singing
there amidst all that snow and ice and wind?

It had to be done, so I sang the great
song of death because I had no place to
go; that was all I knew. When I stumbled
upon the beast, it was asleep.   One round
did the job. "You aren't so big now, are you?"

The Lost Man

They are talking behind my back.

Again, always. That's all right.

The bell tolling tolls for me.

I bring my self into the night.

You can hear the kittens in the sack,

As they drown they hiss and fight --

They go down into the sea;

The knot around the sack is tight.

87 Questions

Do you constantly lose things? Do you lie
and steal and hate other people?   Do you
hate yourself and want to destroy the word
Capitalist?   Can you multi-task and
do you own a phone that you carry with
the rest of your belongings and speak to
at least thirty times a day?   Do you own
a lap-top and are you upgrading each
week?   Do you avoid undesirables?
Do you dress in designer clothing from
Wal-Mart, K-Mart, etc.?   Do you
read books not printed on paper? Do you
love -- but not too much?   I mean: who are you
really?   Speak up.   Don't you know I'd like to get
acquainted so we can come together in some
kind of meaningful way? Please respond soon.

Charles Baudelaire

The thing is dead by the side of the road,
and in the distance clouds filled with anger
grow out of a land named West -- big as God.
I in my place, behind this flat door, a stranger
in a stranger's land, trying not to move
or make a noise that might upset someone --
you know the depth of hatred held in love's
own ulcerated stomach.   Here no fun

exists for long and burial is good
enough to hide the shameful face; those eyes
have seen too much, some of it understood --
dream residue holding to each dawn sky;
Embarrassment, Boredom mount the assault:
there's no time that isn't a time for retreat.

Hart Crane

"The bottom of the sea is cruel."

Given up, and gone, in his explosion
underground -- the mermaid floats away, shuts
her eyes so beautiful, mournful tears drift
and are swallowed by all and any fish
that cruises by this scene / round mouthed and pure
the poet descending into his new room
followed by each magic word he'd put down
with pen onto a sheet of paper, ink
marking the clean surface, a mind
made naked, a world altered beyond all
belief.   And above, between soft blue sky
and wave, the eyes of sailors gaze into
the future tense.   They navigate.   The sail.
They allow old magic to raise them up.

John Berryman

"I'm sorry for those coming. I'm sorry for everyone."

Sometimes things is just no good. The weather
comes. White snow falls, then cold rain and thunder.
The dream unwinds its horrible vision
of a future extinguished. All bridges
fall. How many fall from bridges? Like you.
Like Melissa's friend -- the old guy -- him, too.

Down into traffic oncoming he went.
I can't remember his name. Met him at
a party one time. All of us drunk as
skunks, trying to make the world a better place.
Up all night, we watched for the sun's face
to appear out of our dark land, rise --

cold in an ever-blueing empty belief;
birds awake, air filled with a song called "life".

Paul Celan

"You were my death
you I could hold
when all fell from me."

Forget or deny. Over and out. This
world carries us to our moment, fixes
the time and the space. We live in the air
we are buried in air   we will go there.
The poet is a bitter almond thrown
into history's darkest ditch alone;
the hard mouth forcing speech. What to say?

Words to fill a book, ten books. A gray sky
tells you: "What is sinking without drowning?"
Two feet on dry land. Whose voice is singing?
All this sweetness has been murdered, destroyed --
smoke offered to sky; and April is void
now that our summer will never arrive
and, no -- no. Seasons have little to give.

The Drunk Man

I watched him as he moved along
the sidewalk, as he struggled
along the cracked nightmare below
his feet
dogs barked and cats didn't care
the stars high up above
glimmered through
a mortal distance   he pushed
his bicycle   he could not mount it
push   pause   push again
paused to take a breath
the ground trembles
he had too much   he needed more

We Celebrate

We celebrate the death
the life
of Elvis
in this hot southern
place

this Graceland
we sing the music
that shook the world

it was all very much
more than just a little

all of it belonging
to everyone in the world

look around
nothing is perfect
but go over
to the juke box

look there
"don't be cruel"
"suspicious minds"
"blue moon of kentucky"
"(you aint nothing but a) hound dog"

drop your money in

Sit

Sit, she says, sit.
Stay, stay.
The traffic goes by.
Come, she says, pulls
the leash. They cross
the street.

Later, at home, "Roll
over," the voice says,
and the dog
rolls. "Beg," she says,
"Beg."

The room is quiet.
Outside two men can be
heard talking. Then all
is quiet again.

Because It Never Ends

"Paul." "Paul," they say your name.
On that evening, dark and drizzling,
"Paul," they say. "Yes, yes," I say
beneath the overcast sky, moving
along, bicycle tires hissing, the world
bending its own will into that time.
"Paul," they say from the porch, the
comfortable porch, "Paul," the voices
sing, the day at an end, they have
wine and a dog, they have a house
with yellow walls, they lift their wine
glasses, "Paul," the voices sing,
the dog doesn't move at all, just
sits there at their feet, a greyhound,
tongue wiggling. "Paul": the word
opens the air, "Paul," I am traveling
through this space, this road of
pot-holes, this world of holes,
who are they? "Paul," they say,
lifting their glasses, the world is
almost night, the dog doesn't
move, the street is wet, this is the
song, "Paul, Paul, Paul."

Drift

for my mother

She is in the pain room
and I am gone

her life no longer
is her own

this window cowers
in the gloom

we adjust the
fabricated lens,

a mirror reflecting
space, the space

that cringes, laced
with poison

and there are no friends.

I did not expect this
little, but I know now
what's wrong -- it had

something to do
with a song -- and then

I found my self

inside the middle.

Three

No Crime Was Committed

to Tim Jackson

The 1970's were gone, peace,
love, high school had all ended --
a wide emptiness yawned
over my small town
                    "Rewind,
rewind the son-of-a-bitch,
one more time." That odd car
faded green with one blue
door on the driver's side.

"Godzilla -- oh Godzilla"
we shouted along.
The night around us blinked
with fast food places,
gas stations, traffic lights,
the lights of other cars
going and stopping.

Four of us moving
spasmodic against the dark
car's vinyl upholstery

        "Godzilla, Godzilla"

Feel the guitars plunge
into their own
atomic oblivion, swirl
and chunk and engulfed from
within, without

And no crime was
committed   one day had
simply faded into
another night.   Nothing
was going on but
that wasn't so bad and
we'd drive along
trying to catch maybe
the eye of a car-full
of girls but

the light would always
change someone's
horn would blast
rubber burning
onto asphalt from
some hot-shit's tires
and a beer bottle
smashes in the middle
of an intersection.

        "Godzilla oh oh Godzilla"

Girls scream and laugh
turn off on a side-street,
are gone.   We shout
out the open windows
we wave goodbye to them.

We think we might be crazy
drinking our Mountain Dew
discussing philosophy, poetry

when there are no more words
we turn it up   Those cheap
speakers, rumbling, trembling
vibrating against our ears
our poor ears. Rattling
that became as much a part
of the song as the drum
and its thump -- peace and
love and smiles.

"Son-of-a-bitch   turn it up"

We stop to buy burgers   drive
over to the Fairgrounds
get out and piss
where the sky is bright
with stars.   Then back to it

        "Rewind   Goddamn Godzilla"

The Map Is Uncertain

You remember sitting
up on the roof

Sedalia, Missouri
1978, seventeen years old,
trying to feel

the sun
lost inside the heat

dogs barking
until they stop

lawn mowers
choke on wet grass

your finger is on
the map
it follows what

looks like
a creek or a
river

it flows southward

the sky is hot

the tar softens

you rub your eyes

the river on the map
is going south
it is hot

you climb down
the ladder

walk across
the lawn

fall

a quiet dog
finds you

it will be fine
you know
tomorrow will be fine

The Drunk And His Three-Legged Dog

They were there, then they were gone.
Did they leave in the dead of night?
When I try to remember my memory
fades, my mouth goes dry --
it's hard to swallow. They lived
in that little white house
for many, many years. Once
he'd been married -- there'd been
a wife living with them, but
one night the drunk man
was drunk and angry (so
the story goes) and he picked up
his small hand gun and aimed
the thing at her. Yes, he shot,
he missed her, but his dog --
only wounded, did not die,
of course, but the leg had to go.
She moved back to her mother's
house. After all that you'd see
them walking down the sidewalk:
in the morning, the afternoon,
the evening -- when the weather
allowed. The drunk man weaving
slightly, and the dog limping
along at his side, making the best
of his three legs. Now a sign
in the little white house's front
lawn reads: "For Sale."
It had been a week or more since
I'd seen them out there,
working their way down that

well-worn path. I'm afraid now
if I ask one of the neighbors --
I don't talk much with them
anyway -- I'm afraid they might
tell me something I really
don't want to know.

The Ugly Man

You choose. You were always wrong. In the
rear-view mirrored image of light against
black, or almost black -- your choosing finger
pointed. The carnival surrounded you noisily.
The day of the night. I *want* that. You can't
have that. The ugly man laughs inside the
horrible light and a hand takes your hand and
pulls you away. Step right up. And above,
the crowd of invisible faces swayed and laughed.
Then you were back in your room. There
were little plastic animals -- it was like tele-
vision -- it was the nothing world -- it was
the feeling before the dreams when the light
was turned off by the other hand. It was the
mirror with no one in it. It was the empty lot
filled with a fading memory. A blurred ghost
that nudges you along until you fall -- you are
falling -- you are

Little Yellow Flowers

The little yellow flowers we'd eat
those hot spring days

butterflies   bees
butter scotch

Grandmother cooking fried chicken
lasagna   spaghetti   meat sauce

the laundry drying on the line in
the backyard

nearby catalpa tree with its
long bean sprouts and shade

I'd climb it and sit there alone

that green grass   that blue sky

then go out
circling our block on my bike
timing myself   seeing how far

I'd gone

Teen Age

Turn. Take the turn. Lift the wheel.
The wall is blank and merciful
and embittered. The wolf man
turns his dreams into tomorrows.
The miles rear view reflected prove
an essential form of context. Push
the 8-Track into the opening darkness.
Led Zepplin. Physical Graffiti, an
album many critics at its release
disliked. I don't know. I like it.
The music rumbled shaky out of the
cheap speakers. It was the night
that spread out all across the small
town, all over the world. Going
past all those places, those blank
walls, your eye-sight would be
stolen briefly -- the drum beat pushed
it all forward, along, ahead, it seemed,
of everyone else. Open another
can of Schlitz, fucker, the world
belongs to you.

My Grandfather's Accident

"Goddamn Son Of A Bitch,"
he screamed
and I was in the house
that little pink house on Harrison
and my Grandmother
was in the house, too,
and we ran outside -- blood on the driveway
and one of his shoes
had been ripped apart
he'd stepped into
the action of a lawn mower's blade,
dancing on one foot
leaning onto our car
"Goddamn it, Goddamn it"
blood coming out
of his shoe, blood on the grass
the drive-way -- he danced in pain
he hit the car with his fist
the push mower
flipped there on its side,
still running
it was hot and August
and the summer was almost over
so they climbed into the car
my grandmother and grandfather
and off they went to the hospital
where someone would stitch up
his foot
no toes were lost
he'd been wearing good shoes
and the summer was almost over

Together

Come together. Out on the wire.
Coming together. A mythic time long
ago. Resplendent. Cause and effect.
No thought on the hill over-looking
the valley. Biological tumult. The
belief is the end of the begining. Through
hook and crookedness. Finding your self
in the middle of nothing. The nothing
in the center of a belief that has no
basis in what has proven to
be -- the hard factual evidence --
the dance where the accidental
exorcises its tangential body politic --
crucible of shamelessness
buried in the slang of desire.
Devices impinging with brutal
deftness, words half-baked --
lost in the evolutionary day-dream --
witch hands that have clutched
magically informed excess, held
it all up to our eyes -- hooked us
into the magnetic pole -- pulled
North and up and there it is
with the voice on the rise
going beyond where it really
needed to go.

October

I like the way the voices

keep going   won't stop

into the night   the words

unspool   but only now

and then can I understand

any given utterance   English

Spanish   who knows

it all pours out and keeps

coming   I don't care   I

know everything will be

fine   they will go to sleep

and I will too   white

noise   all it becomes

not exactly real   here as I

lean over and turn out

the light

The Window Washer

He dangles from a rope, a few ropes,
tan arms stretching out,
pushes the squeegee back and forth
over the glass surface   swings
here and there, works his way
to solid ground   work day over
he goes home where he falls to
sleep. He dreams of dark hallways,
attic rooms, mummies inside their
boxes. He dreams of being shot
out of a cannon into a crowd of
lonely daffodils. He dreams that his
eyes turn to stone. He dreams a
dark friend conspires to do him
harm. They want his job. His life
will soon belong to the one who
never dreams.

Kung Fu From Beyond The Grave

It took a long time

to get there

to become and then unbecome

lost in a world

where words have failed us

a plateau of bad decisions

as if life were taking place

the dust blows down

an empty street

until there is no more

blue in the sky

only a brown palette

smeared over landscape

placed there by an artist

in his lost room

dreaming funny stuff

The Trees Fight The Sky

after the storm
after this storm
trees fight the sky

they pull no punches
on this afternoon
green and milky white

thunder faded now
radio in the next room
delivers the news

nature in violence
with nature
the leaves sharp

the stiff limbs
whip away
a sky blue sky

slice through air

how those roots
beneath feet of dirt
grow off

toward a dark future

the dreams
I had last night
are gone

Lyric

I do not know   I do not
know   I do not

forget it   maybe you
know   maybe you

know something
from that special place

turned onto the real truth
that is the only

truth circulating
in the vicinity of

the people of this
world where death and

life cross paths
on a daily basis

mutilated belief
stinks in any can

where trash has found
a temporary home

The Guilty

Maybe he did it, maybe he didn't.
Who cares? He walked in black
and white along the empty street,
walls of fog spill in from the river,
a thick dampness settles on every
inch of that town. His eyes lost
in shadow, deep inside a floating
life. Milky air drifts up until
huge buildings fade out.

He wants out, but can't seem
to manage it. The shop windows,
the parked cars, the puddle of
water: all expose him for what
he is. A cigarette seems to
light itself, smoke rises, mingles,
pushes its way up. Who cares?
He either did it or he didn't.
Now go on, go on home, and
mind your own business.

2 November 2015

Walking down Pirates Alley
toward Jackson Square

the baby snake has escaped
and the man with the cup

is trying to reclaim
the reptile

get it back into the cup
not get bit in the process

the snake was frightened
and angry

it tried to bite him

"Hey, man, how much
you give me for this guy?"

"No, no -- I don't need
a snake," I said

I walked away out on
Jackson Square and someone

was screaming "fuck"
"Fuck, fuck, fuck," they screamed

Lament

I forgot about
yesterday
my hand in front of my eyes
Yeats' birthday today
the inside and
outside
we dig for
the forgotten
tiny histories
exposed
our curiosity kills
rain falling
will destroy rock
god is punished
in book after book
rain dropped
into the river
floods
poetry
turns around
is as useless
as a cliche
but that is wrong
it swells in flow and churns
around impediment
the hand in the bell tower
pulls the warning
you can hear the iron clang
resound and you
know all
you need to know

Doomsday Clock Now
Three Minutes to Midnight

(23 January 2015)

On this rainy day, this overcast, wet, cold
day, cold enough day, New Orleans winter
day, cars on La Salle shoosh by on the wet
asphalt. I've eaten chili for lunch, chili
made two days ago -- hamburger, canned
tomatoes and corn, green pepper, squash,
garlic, jalapenos, spices. I'm sitting down
to write this about the doomsday clock being
moved ahead two minutes as I wait for the hot
water to come back on -- I'd called them about
an hour ago and was told after being on hold
for quite some time that the problem should
be taken care of later today. "Thank you
very much," I said. After that I went out to
check the mail and found a short note clinging
to my apartment's front door. It was the third
note of its kind, saying exactly the same thing
the previous note said: "The rental office will
no longer be accepting cash -- only money
orders or cashiers checks" -- and in large print --
"NO PERSONAL CHECKS WILL BE
ACCEPTED" and ended wishing me "Happy
Holidays." The only piece of mail in the box
was a card: Sex Offender Notification:
age 48   sex Male   race White   height 5' 9"
weight 170   Hair and eyes both Brown
Tattoos   one a Fleur de Lis and the other
a Penguin with a Plunger   Description of crime
involved material dealing with the sexual

exploitation of minors. I put the card some
place where I wouldn't lose it; then decided
it was cold enough to turn on the heater for
a little while. And then I read the article about
the Doomsday Clock and how the atomic
scientists have decided to move it up two
minutes making it now three minutes until
that mythic time Wilson Pickett once sang
about waiting until -- that hushed and personal
moment in the darkness when love and lust
mingled, tumbled down -- two minutes
closer now as the ice melts, the oceans die,
the bombs wait in concrete steel holding
cells -- dried river banks, forests on fire,
tuskless elephant bodies, tornado, hurricane --
one-hundred and eighty seconds unless
someone does something, and who knows,
maybe it could already be too late.

>"I'm gonna wait 'til the Midnight Hour
>when there's no one else around . . ."

Wilson Pickett singing long ago as I drove my
way through late night streets of the small
town where I was born. Wicked Pickett on
the 8-Track machine screaming out his soul
from those cheap little speakers in back. I
was driving around in circles, looking
out the windshield at the dark landscape
falling behind me. And once that song ended --
horns fading away -- I guess it was just time
to go home and go to sleep.

Live To Forget

(A Prayer For Johnny Mancuso)

What we can do is what we are doing
as the parade outside the bar goes by
down Chartres Street the marching band
and the conventioneers they wave
beads given them to wave
two stilt walkers wobble to the music
here we are all almost down by the riverside
"Welcome, welcome to New Orleans --"
Yes, yes, yes, home of Johnny Mancuso
and many others, crazy here and out
in the elements of any given evening
as the sun turns a blind eye mercifully
away from the poor, suffering fools
here in the barroom's plenitude
of shadows. Johnny Mancuso says
"Pray for me, pray for me,"
cigarette ready for match between
two fingers, right hand, a beer
on the table, open, ready for
the taking.

Castle Of Monsters

I don't care who you are
who you happen to
be or not
be   I can forget
the incidents that have
brought this
vile innuendo
let's separate the blood
from the wine   turn
our cheeks around
and let the horror
disperse
in this song
our mouths opening
have exposed since
the day time
began   and space
created horizon
a thing we tried
to measure ourselves
against   and
failing
were
swallowed

Tomorrow Shoes

The dream that infects you

beyond what you believe

life might be

behold there must

there has to be

more than those elements

obvious to the eye

or vision's edge

where no explanation

resolves itself

and passes through

the straightened narrow

a crack in your doorway

blooming with this

sudden passionate resolve

unable to predict what

destruction might be

unleashed in any given

backyard shady grove

where the neighbors

mumble their way into

another eight hours of sleep

before the sun comes up

and the chickens squawk

out by the crooked fence

dreams everywhere

falling down

Vision

Two observers are walking back
to a car in a small parking lot

after they'd spent the last two hours
watching a movie, the mid-afternoon's sun

dresses the sky with a wide blueness,
empty and pure.

Whatever it was they were talking
about has been long forgotten.

Maybe it was the movie   the movie
also lost now in time   when

one of them sees it, in the flat distance,
thirty or forty parking spaces

away   the sparsely filled lot
held little resistance

to the shopping cart, its four
wobbly wheels, the clatter

as it approached, slow at first,
then gaining speed, metallic

clicking, over the summer hot
black-top, free of human

hands: it had grown wings, it was ready.

For Dave

He opened up the guts
displaying the eternal
stratagem uncoiling its
path towards the light

He wouldn't let go
his mouth would move
and the words built
a response to the sun's ritual appearance

He swallowed birds and stood
naked above the chasm
careless and full of love
full of tragic relief

He knew that I would write
these words   buried as we all
are in the future's soggy pit
that I would write these words to him

French Quarter Sketch

The man speaking to his hand
what is he saying there beneath
that building's eve protecting
him from a mid noon's
heat   traffic passing by
a few feet away

3 cigarette packs arranged
within his reach, a lighter,
and some packs of matches,
just in case.

What does his hand say back
to him through that intimate
space   pedestrian traffic
on the move, going, going.

He has no four walls
to hide behind
or if he does, then
sometimes he just goes
out   to smoke and
sit on the sidewalk

with the music of
slow traffic feet away,
and the hot noon heat, and
the people with their dogs
on leashes.

The Fishing Pole

They used to walk along country roads. Whistle that
carefree tune. At least on tv they used to walk those dirt
roads, whistling. Whistle a carefree tune. I was walking
down one of those roads once. Cameras following me,
followed me at some distance, slowly tracking closer.
The tune I was whistling wasn't one that you might
easily recognize -- just a sound collage rooted in those
emotional strains from this or that moment from my
past. Did I mention the fishing pole in my hand? I
had one and I carried it rifle-like over my right shoulder.
The pole was symbolic: my life, my time, my world.
There was no line, I had no bait. As I walked along
the camera came closer and closer. The man I assumed
to be the Director was shuffling along, gesturing with his
fat hands. "This is going no where," he said angrily,
"what do you think you're doing?"
"What do you want me to do?" I asked.
"You need to project, PRO-ject -- you need to move
the plot forward." I thought for a moment.
"I am a human being," I said.
"That's good, that's good," he said, excited.
"I have, I have a purpose on this road. I will keep
moving until I arrive."
"Great, that's more like it."
"I am going out to meet my destiny."
"Marvelous," the Director exalted.
I gazed of toward the direction I'd been walking.
"Pardon me," I said, "I must be going now." The camera,
the camera man, and the Director pulled back, receded
into the near distance. I thought now it was a good idea
to give up the whistling. Time to get serious.

Bigfoot At 55

"You have to keep revenging your heart."
                    -- Professor Irwin Corey
(or did he say: "You have to keep revenge in your heart")

No good news, really. For the world. Same old
earthquakes and bombings. I was bitten by
something the other day. I hope it isn't
serious. Time will tell. The man next door
hammers away at an object. It sounds
wooden or hollow. Huge clouds migrating
in silence, move from the west to the east. Rain
is being called for tomorrow. I have
no faith in their system. It might rain; it
might not. Yesterday I went into town.
The avenues were clogged. I ate something
somewhere and then returned home. I unlocked
the stubborn door, walked into the bedroom,
and sat down. No one was there. But me.

The Trick

We did the trick
the plug was pulled
here is our negative space
a decisively empty pocket
gas tank majesty upheld
your fly paper reveals all

We did the trick
as laughter pushed out tears
this insect abandon pauses
easy circumference adjust
arms with deadened hands
try uselessly to hug

We did the trick
the audience was inconslusive
there was no ovation
standing or otherwise
it was a long ride
back to the dressing room

Neighbors

They will sit there forever. Across the street.
Facing each other. Blankets of rain
curtain the world. The front porch
frames the two in profile as they discuss
the events of the day. Dogs run by
in the street out front. Children's
voices will be heard crackling from
around the corner. The sun continues
to hide away behind the brick walls.
A large bucket filled with non-descript
flowers divides the space between them.
Far off, and above it all, there is
no way that you can breathe or live.
The stars twinkling cold knife you good.

What Do You Want

"What do you want from mewhat do you want
from me   what do you want from me . . ." she sang
as she rode her bicycle down the dark street this first day
of December and the night was stil and warm at 7:30.
We were on Chartres Street moving along with the river
that moved along over there to our right. I felt like I was
no one as I listened to the woman's voice some place
not far behind me. What did anyone want from anyone?
We all want something. We want good music to listen to,
perhaps. We want a clear night still warm at the beginning
of December. What else is there? Bombs explode.
War and murder span our decades.
The moon is sick of us.

We really should go elsewhere. To a land where peace
is free and the morning licks our toes. Forget how bad
feet stink as night ticks and tocks away. The memory
of bombs. "What do you want from me"
The landscape is without sound. Below and above.
She becomes operatic as she glides down Chartres,
glides through these shadows:
"What do you want from me"   I try to keep my distance.
The sound of her words follows me. This December place
holds itself in the wet air trying to explain all of what isn't
understood to the people who just don't care. And I turn off
on some dark street, going north, and her voice, so pure,
keeps going straight down river, toward the Gulf.

Godzilla Is Dead

What are we   you me   what   what   where
the heavy sofa by the road's hard side
the words that don't mean what they mean
say something else   mankind and movement
talking paranoia hazard   listen to the
sound behind the dark window thump
what and where   all places at once avalanche
construct unknowable worlds   above below
quit the diatribe   bring the smashed
day's end to a close   you have taken the
bath   plump babe   in the sink   it was
August   they take the picture   only years
can do this to us   out in the front yard
up in the sky   a scream lost in fire
concludes our last and only act

The Sun Light In Her Hair, His Tattooed Arms

They got on the bus

the sun was going down

he had a garbage bag

with what sounded like

several metal objects inside

the ravens swirled

through November air

busy settling down

in the coming night

she could hardly walk

or stumble as she found

the plastic bus seat

her friend was busy

with a phone to his face

talking   explaining their situation

she wore a purple tank top

a padded bra

exposed breast

cleavage beneath

leaning there in

the last of the day's sun

as the guy she's with

talks on

and when she is about to collapse

into the aisle

he slaps her across the knee

she wakes and looks around

as if she knew where she was

and what was going on

but as soon as her eyes open

they close again

with the last light of the evening

spilling through bus windows

and the talk of the people

around us

their words collapsed

impossible

I looked into the space

between her breasts

beneath the padded bra

as she sits up

for that moment

and then slumps

eyes closed

forward

her escort talking

into the void

about money

and things

about the plastic bag

at his feet

then she is going down

again

down

and the man with the bag

slaps her two or three more times

then she says

"If you do that again . . ."

and I couldn't hear the rest

of what she said

and he just keeps talking

and time passed

and I looked

out the window

at the evening

sky growing dim

all around us

then the bus driver

says something to her

as she almost falls

and she tells the bus driver

that she is high as fuck

and that was that --

the two got off

at my stop

and I watched them disappear

with the sound

of the bus

and highway

and the birds

hiding in trees.

Letter My Mother Kept

I found it one day by accident. The letter my
mother kept in a shoe box in the closet -- those thin

pages, folded pieces of yellow stationery, discovered on
the highest shelf. Outside the rain was coming down.

My father's voice, his words to my mother from
a Kansas City hotel room -- four pages, five

pages, six? Begging her to love him the way he
believed she'd once loved him. I read that letter

twice, put it back into the box, -- pushed
those words back into their musty place.

The Monkees

Here we have a kind of imperfect purity, a thing
already lost before it was discovered. Day dreams
of Saturday afternoons that pull you into them
and allow you to be filled with light, carefreeness
that lifts every bit of you out of the routine,
the dreaded daily grind -- school or job -- sets you
free to wander along sunny streets with no thought
other than the heavy realization that some of the
universe can be in touch with you, your joyous
heart that leaps within the chest -- and there is no
target at which this fluidity is aimed -- the air is
a jumping off point, and it fills you as you beam
outward to anyone you happen to meet. Smile.
Say "Hello."   From this position a new kind of
place in the midst of meaninglessness -- the abyss
will never be overwhelmed, but you will make the
leap over this chasm and the dream of being
a dreamer -- a day dream believer -- will hold you
by the hand always.

300 Years

Night had just arrived
it was a cool evening
end of a work day
the back and forth laughter
conversations drift in and out
about two blocks away
maybe down by the river
sound of bag-pipes rises up
and if the wind shifts just right
you can detect
the stench of Bourbon Street

And I am there on that corner
again   a place wedged
somehow into my eternal
nature   can of beer
in hand   watching the silhouettes
walk in and out
of the grocery store
waiting for the time
to come   the time when
I can leave

and there they were

three of them
sniffing at the cool air --
three baby rats
edging out of the sewer's
mouth   bathed in yellow
grocery store light

This odd city
three-hundred-years old
city of the drunken night
city of hangover
all of it   soon enough exposed
by that clockwork sun

a few tourists walk past
no one sees the little
eyes blinking   looking

examining this other new world.

Special Thanks to the following for their friendship and inspiration: Ron Cowan, Debbie Nolan, Rhonda Chalfant, Robert C. Jones, Walter Bargen, Sherod Santos, Randy McCleary, Frank Miranti, Lesle Forbes, Cain Burdeau, Dave Brinks & the Gold Mine, Lee Grue Metzen, Delia Nakayama, Peter Nu, Randy Bowlin, Mark Satterwhite, Sara Cleaveland, Richard Simpson, Reddog, the Tullis family, Nancy Harris, Mike True, Thaddeus Conti, Charlotte Mears, and all the folks at the Maple Leaf Poetry gathering.

58792559R00088

Made in the USA
Columbia, SC
25 May 2019